Explore Space!

Mae Jemison

by Thomas Streissguth

Consultant:
James Gerard
Aerospace Education Specialist
NASA Aerospace Education Services Program

Bridgestone Books
an imprint of Capstone Press
Mankato, Minnesota

Bridgestone Books are published by Capstone Press
151 Good Counsel Drive, P.O. Box 669, Mankato, Minnesota 56002
http://www.capstone-press.com

Library of Congress Cataloging-in-Publication Data
Streissguth, Thomas, 1958–
   Mae Jemison / by Thomas Streissguth.
   p. cm.—(Explore space!)
   Summary: Presents a brief biography of the first African-American woman to travel
into space.
   Includes bibliographical references and index.
   ISBN 0-7368-1626-7 (hardcover)
   1. Jemison, Mae, 1956– —Juvenile literature. 2. African American women astronauts—
Biography—Juvenile literature. 3. Astronauts—United States—Biography—Juvenile
literature. [1. Jemison, Mae, 1956– 2. Astronauts. 3. African Americans—Biography.
4. Women—Biography.] I. Title. II. Series.
TL789.85.J46 .S77 2003
629.45'0092—dc21   2002010137

Editorial Credits

Chris Harbo and Roberta Schmidt, editors; Karen Risch, product planning editor; Steve
   Christensen, series designer; Juliette Peters, cover and interior designer; Alta Schaffer,
   photo researcher

Photo Credits

Corbis/Bettmann, 6
Corbis Saba/Marc Asnin, 18
Mark Regan Photography, 20
NASA, cover, 4, 8, 10, 12, 14, 16

1 2 3 4 5 6 08 07 06 05 04 03

Table of Contents

Mae Jemison

Mae Jemison was the first African American woman to travel into space. She flew in the space shuttle *Endeavour* on September 12, 1992. Mae and six other astronauts did 43 tests in space. They used a laboratory called Spacelab-J for the experiments.

laboratory
a place where people do experiments to learn new things

Mae worked as a doctor in Los Angeles before she became an astronaut.

Doctor from Chicago

Mae Carol Jemison was born October 17, 1956, in Decatur, Alabama. Mae's family soon moved to Chicago, Illinois. Her father was a carpenter. Mae's mother was a teacher. After high school, Mae studied medicine. In 1981, she graduated from Cornell Medical College.

graduate
to finish all required classes at a school

Sally Ride went into space on June 18, 1983. She was a member of the second *Challenger* mission. Sally served as a mission specialist during the flight.

Dreams of Becoming an Astronaut

In 1983, Mae joined the Peace Corps. She worked as a doctor in Africa. That same year, Sally Ride became the first U.S. woman to travel into space. Mae dreamed of becoming an astronaut too. In 1985, Mae applied for NASA's astronaut training program.

Peace Corps
a group that helps people in other countries

9

Challenger exploded 73 seconds after liftoff. NASA stopped launching space shuttles for two years after the disaster.

The *Challenger* Disaster

More than 2,000 people applied to be astronauts in 1985. Then a terrible accident happened. On January 28, 1986, the space shuttle *Challenger* exploded. The accident killed seven astronauts. NASA's astronaut program stopped until October, 1986.

The KC-135 aircraft climbs and dives to create the feeling of zero gravity. Over the years, astronauts have nicknamed the plane the Vomit Comet. Feeling weightless can make some people feel sick.

Passing the Tests

In October, 1986, Mae again applied to be an astronaut. NASA chose her for the astronaut program in 1987. She trained and exercised every day. Mae also flew in NASA's KC-135 aircraft. This plane helped her get ready to be weightless in space.

weightless
free of the pull of gravity

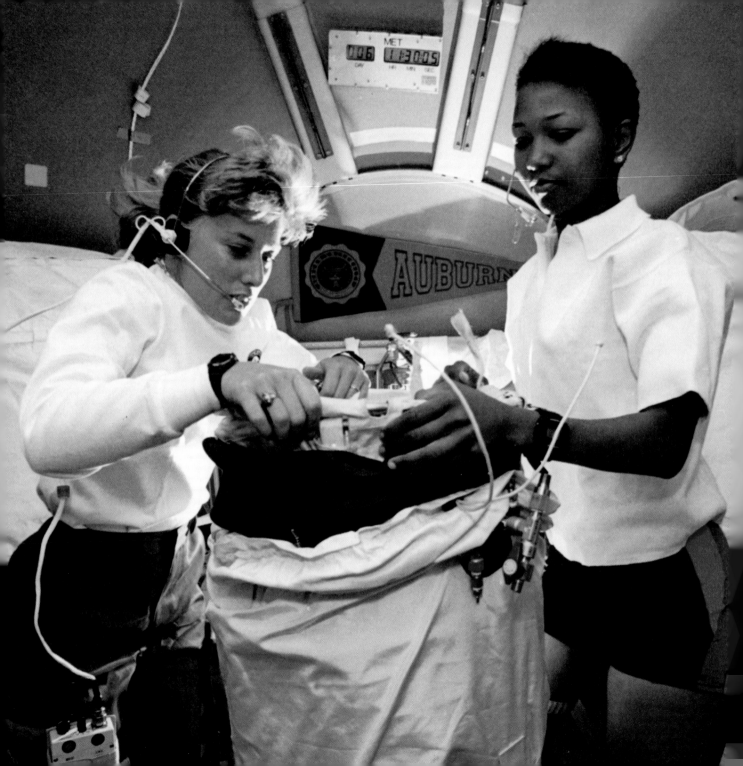

The Flight of *Endeavour*

On September 12, 1992, Mae traveled into space aboard the space shuttle *Endeavour*. Mae did many experiments inside *Endeavour's* Spacelab-J. She tested the effects of weightlessness on people and animals. Mae used frogs, fish, and fruit flies in some of her experiments.

Endeavour's **Crew**

Endeavour's crew worked together to make the mission successful. The crew split into a red team and a blue team. These teams did science tests all day and night in Spacelab-J. Crew members helped Mae with many of her experiments.

After the Flight

After *Endeavour's* flight, Mae left NASA. She began to teach classes at Dartmouth College in 1993. Mae also formed the Jemison Group. This company helps poor countries use new medical equipment. Some equipment helps doctors talk to people in hard-to-reach areas.

Science Camp

In 1994, Mae started The Earth We
Share science camp in Houston, Texas.
Students between the ages of 12 and
16 can attend. They learn how to do
science experiments. Students also
learn how to use science to solve
common problems.

Important Dates

1956—Mae Carol Jemison is born October 17 in Decatur, Alabama.

1981—Mae graduates as a doctor from Cornell Medical College.

1983—Mae joins the Peace Corps and travels to Sierra Leone and Liberia in Africa.

1985—Mae applies for NASA's astronaut training program.

1992—Mae flies aboard the *Endeavour*. She and the crew perform 43 experiments in *Endeavour's* Spacelab-J.

1993—Mae becomes a teacher at Dartmouth College and starts the Jemison Group.

1994—Mae starts The Earth We Share science camp for students.

Present—Mae lives in Houston, Texas.

Words to Know

astronaut (ASS-truh-nawt)—someone trained to fly into space in a spacecraft

experiment (ek-SPER-uh-ment)—a test to learn something new

graduate (GRAJ-oo-ate)—to finish all required classes at a school

gravity (GRAV-uh-tee)—a force that pulls objects together; gravity pulls objects down toward the center of Earth.

laboratory (LAB-ruh-tor-ee)—a place where people do experiments to learn new things

mission (MISH-uhn)—a planned job or task

space shuttle (SPAYSS SHUHT-uhl)—a spacecraft that can fly into space and return to Earth many times

weightless (WATE-liss)—free of the pull of gravity

Read More

Gelletly, LeeAnne. *Mae Jemison.* Women of Achievement. Philadelphia: Chelsea House Publishers, 2002.

Naden, Corinne J., and Rose Blue. *Mae Jemison: Out of this World.* Gateway Biography. Brookfield, Conn: The Millbrook Press, 2003.

Internet Sites

Track down many sites about Mae Jemison.
Visit the FACT HOUND at
http://www.facthound.com

IT IS EASY! IT IS FUN!

1) Go to *http://www.facthound.com*
2) Type in: 0736816267
3) Click on "FETCH IT" and FACT HOUND will find several links hand-picked by our editors.

Relax and let our pal FACT HOUND do the research for you!

Index